THE USBORNE
SECOND WORLD WAR
STICKER BOOK

Henry Brook and Hazel Maskell

Illustrated by Ian McNee

Designed by Tom Lalonde
with Samantha Barrett and Stephen Moncrieff

Edited by Jane Chisholm and Conrad Mason

Consultant: Terry Charman, Historian, Imperial War Museum

Contents

With thanks to Madeleine James

SCHOLASTIC INC.
New York Toronto London Auckland
Sydney Mexico City New Delhi Hong Kong

Fighter planes

The Second World War was fought on land, at sea and in the air. Fighter pilots duelled for control of the skies in lethal high-speed flying machines.

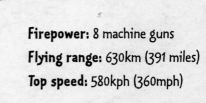

British Supermarine Spitfire

The Spitfire became the most famous Second World War fighter plane in the Royal Air Force. With wide, oval wings and a sleek design, it was faster and more agile than the German *Luftwaffe*'s champion fighter, the Bf 109. Powerful machine guns were mounted in its wings.

Firepower: 8 machine guns
Flying range: 630km (391 miles)
Top speed: 580kph (360mph)

Symbol displayed on RAF planes

British Hawker Hurricane

Firepower: 8 machine guns
Flying range: 965km (600 miles)
Top speed: 530kph (329mph)

The Hurricane wasn't as fast or acrobatic as the Spitfire, but it was tougher and more reliable. A Hurricane could be shot up badly and still limp back to base, to be patched up for another mission.

Hurricanes were so tough that one managed to cut through the tail of a German bomber with its wing.

German Messerschmitt Bf 109

Firepower: 1 cannon, 2 machine guns
Flying range: 665km (413 miles)
Top speed: 570kph (354mph)

The 109 was a great fighter plane – small and light with a shell-firing cannon – but it had a short range. By the time pilots arrived in Britain, they only had 15 minutes to fight before they had to head back over the English Channel to refuel.

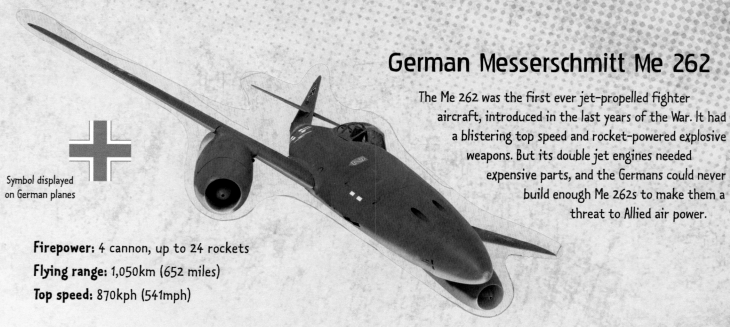

German Messerschmitt Me 262

The Me 262 was the first ever jet-propelled fighter aircraft, introduced in the last years of the War. It had a blistering top speed and rocket-powered explosive weapons. But its double jet engines needed expensive parts, and the Germans could never build enough Me 262s to make them a threat to Allied air power.

Firepower: 4 cannon, up to 24 rockets

Flying range: 1,050km (652 miles)

Top speed: 870kph (541mph)

Symbol displayed on German planes

American P-51D Mustang

Firepower: 6 machine guns

Flying range: 1,830km (1,137 miles)

Top speed: 710kph (441mph)

Early Mustangs couldn't fly very well at great heights, but once they were refitted with new engines, these planes had few rivals. Mustangs could easily outpace Bf 109s and had enough range to act as fighter escorts for US bombers over Germany and Japan.

Symbol displayed on US planes

Japanese Mitsubishi A6M Zero

In December 1941, Zero fighters took part in the raid on the US Pacific fleet at Pearl Harbor.

Firepower: 2 cannon, 2 machine guns

Flying range: 2,970km (1,845 miles)

Top speed: 533kph (331mph)

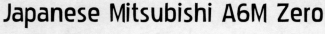

Symbol displayed on Japanese planes

Designed to be launched from aircraft carriers, the Zero was light and could fly huge distances without having to refuel. Early models had folding wing tips to make them easier to store side-by-side. The Zero could also carry a heavy bomb.

Bombers

In the dead of night, long-range aircraft on both sides pounded enemy factories with bombs, and brought terror to cities hundreds of miles from any battlefield. Late in the War, daytime bomber raids reduced whole cities to rubble and ash.

British de Havilland Mosquito

Crew: 2

Firepower: 4 cannon, 4 machine guns

Bombload: 1,800kg (3,968lb)

Wingspan: 16.5m (54ft)

Flying range: 2,400km (1,491 miles)

Top speed: 640kph (398mph)

Built of plywood to keep its weight down, the twin-engined "Timber Terror" could outpace most attackers. Wood didn't show up on wartime radar equipment, so the plane was often used for low-flying shock bombing raids at tree-top height.

German Junkers Ju 87 "the Stuka"

With wings shaped like a gull's and large undercarriage wheels, the Stuka (short for *Sturzkampfflugzeug*, meaning "dive-bomber") looked an awkward flying machine. But this odd design kept the plane steady in a vertical dive, making the Stuka a precision bomber.

Undercarriage wheels

German pilots fitted sirens to their Stukas. These sirens howled during the dive, spreading panic among troops and civilians on the ground.

Crew: 2

Firepower: 3 machine guns

Bombload: 700kg (1,543lb)

Wingspan: 14m (46ft)

Flying range: 1,500km (932 miles)

Top speed: 410kph (255mph) cruising, 600kph (373mph) in dive

British Fairey Swordfish

With its double set of wings, the Fairey Swordfish biplane resembled the lumbering fighters of the First World War. But this tough torpedo bomber helped destroy enemy warships and U-boats – German submarines – right through the War.

Crew: 3

Firepower: 8 machine guns

Bombload: single torpedo, sea mine or 2 bombs

Wingspan: 14m (46ft)

Flying range: 630km (391 miles)

Top speed: 580kph (360mph)

Turret

British Avro Lancaster MkIII

Crew: 7

Firepower: 8 machine guns

Bombload: 9,000kg (19,842lb)

Wingspan: 31m (102ft)

Flying range: 4,000km (2,485 miles)

Top speed: 430kph (267mph)

The Lancaster could carry almost its own weight in explosives. Its gun crew had to sit in special turrets built into the plane's fuselage (main body), and some got frostbite after flying for hours in freezing temperatures.

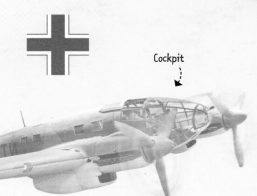

Lancasters were used in the "Dambuster raids" of 1943, when they dropped bouncing bombs on three German dams in a night-time attack.

German Heinkel He 111

The Heinkel He 111 was a medium-sized bomber. It had a glazed nose section for its cockpit (the pilot's control area), which some air crews said made it feel as if they were flying in a greenhouse.

Cockpit

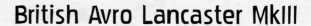

Crew: 5

Firepower: 1 cannon, 8 machine guns

Bombload: 2,000kg (4,409lb)

Wingspan: 23m (75ft)

Flying range: 2,000km (1,243 miles)

Top speed: 435kph (270mph)

American Boeing B-17G Flying Fortress

Crew: 10

Firepower: 13 machine guns

Bombload: up to 3,000kg (6,614lb)

Wingspan: 32m (105ft)

Flying range: 3,000km (1,864 miles)

Top speed: 460kph (286mph)

Designed as a heavy bomber for daylight raids, the massive B-17 had plenty of machine guns to fight off enemy planes. But even with this firepower, over 5,000 B-17s were lost in combat missions.

Allied tanks

The perfect tank is fast, tough and armed with a big gun, but it can be difficult to combine these strengths in one. Allied tank designers built a lot of vehicles during the Second World War, but none were as powerful as the largest German machines.

Allied tanks race onto French beaches on D-Day.

American Sherman M4 Medium Tank

Crew: 5
Guns: 75mm (3") diameter main cannon, 2 machine guns
Speed: 40kph (25mph)
Hull thickness: 65mm (2.6")

The Sherman tank had lots of faults. Its firepower was poor, its engine was too loud, its hull (main body) protection was too weak and it had a nasty habit of catching fire when hit.

But it was a cheap and versatile tank, and its firepower was improved as the war went on.

Symbol displayed on US tanks

Russian T-34 Medium Tank

Crew: 4
Guns: 76mm (3") main cannon, 2 machine guns
Speed: 40kph (25mph)
Hull thickness: 65mm (2.6")

Symbol displayed on Soviet tanks

German forces were stopped in their tracks by the power, speed and mobility of the Russian T-34. It was cheap to produce and crudely built, but it could cover the roughest ground and take on any German tank.

T-34s were very easy to construct. By 1942, most were built by inexperienced workers – women, old men and young boys.

Russian JS-2 Heavy Tank

Crew: 4

Guns: 122mm (4.8") cannon, 3 machine guns

Speed: 37kph (23mph)

Hull thickness: 120mm (4.7")

The JS-2 – named after the Soviet leader, Josef Stalin – was a fearsome machine, with the biggest gun of any tank on the battlefield. It was built late in the war, and helped Stalin's forces on their last advance into Germany.

Symbol displayed
on French tanks

French Char B1 bis Heavy Tank

Crew: 4

Guns: 2 shell-firing cannon, 2 machine guns

Speed: 28kph (17mph)

Hull thickness: 60mm (2.4")

This tank was strong and heavy, but too slow and cumbersome to keep up with the speedy German tanks it faced during the invasion of France in 1940.

British A12 Infantry Tank, Matilda II

Crew: 4

Guns: small main cannon, 1 machine gun

Speed: 13kph (8mph)

Hull thickness: 78mm (3.1")

This small tank was designed to support slow infantry attacks over rough ground. It was used against Italian and German tanks in North Africa.

In some desert battles, British soldiers called a truce in the afternoon so they could "brew up" some tea.

American M26 Pershing Heavy Tank

Crew: 5

Guns: 90mm (3.5") cannon, 3 machine guns

Speed: 48kph (30mph)

Hull thickness: 102mm (4")

The Pershing had a large gun, and was nicknamed the "Tiger Tamer" after the huge German "Tiger" tanks it was built to destroy. It was one of the first tanks that could shoot on the move. Most other tanks had to stop to aim accurately.

Axis tanks

The Germans produced the best tanks of all the Axis Powers. But, in the end, the quality was no match for the vast quantity of tanks built by the Allies.

German troops, tanks and planes go forward during a lightning-fast *Blitzkrieg* attack.

Panzerkampfwagen II Light Tank

Crew: 3

Guns: light cannon, 1 machine gun

Speed: 40kph (25mph)

Hull thickness: 35mm (1.4")

Symbol displayed on German tanks

This *Panzerkampfwagen* (which means "tank" in German), or Panzer, was built for rapid strikes and scouting missions rather than heavy fighting. Its cannon could barely dent the hulls of most Allied tanks, so it was used less and less as the War went on.

Italian Carro Armato M13/40 Medium Tank

Crew: 4

Guns: light cannon, 3–4 machine guns

Speed: 32kph (20mph)

Hull thickness: 42mm (1.7")

These Italian tanks were too light to stand up to the British Matildas they encountered in the deserts of North Africa. They were poorly equipped, and often had no radios. Some crews attached sandbags to the outside of the tank, to improve its protection.

Panzer IV Medium Tank

Crew: 5

Guns: 75mm (3") cannon, 2 machine guns

Speed: 40kph (25mph)

Hull thickness: 50mm (2")

Much tougher than previous Panzers, these tanks led the German advance into Russia in 1941. They were in production until the end of the War, regularly updated with bigger guns and thicker metal protection.

Japanese Type 95 Ha-Go Light Tank

Crew: 3

Guns: 37mm (1.5") cannon, 2 machine guns

Speed: 45kph (28mph)

Hull thickness: 12mm (0.5")

Symbol displayed on Japanese tanks

Ha-Go tanks often operated in thick jungles in southeast Asia.

Japanese tanks were too poorly protected, with very thin hulls, to rival Allied machines they encountered in southeast Asia. The three-man crew in a Type 95 had too many jobs to do — driving, loading, aiming and commanding — which made the tank hard to control in battle.

Panzer V "Panther" Heavy Tank

Crew: 5

Guns: 75mm (3") cannon, 2 machine guns

Speed: 46kph (29mph)

Hull thickness: 100mm (3.9")

The Panther was designed to tackle tough Soviet tanks like the T-34. It was a great all-rounder, fast and strong, and not as difficult to manufacture as later Panzers.

Panzer VI "Tiger 2" Heavy Tank

Crew: 5

Guns: 88mm (3.5") cannon, 2 machine guns

Speed: 42kph (26mph)

Hull thickness: 180mm (7.1")

The Tiger 2 was too heavy for most bridges to bear, so it had to cross rivers and streams at shallow points.

The Tiger 2 was a gigantic machine with a gun that could knock out other tanks at great distances. It had a very thick hull, but needed huge amounts of fuel. It was built very late in the War, and only a few hundred fought in battle.

Army vehicles

Armies in the Second World War relied on a range of vehicles to move men, weapons and supplies into the thick of the fighting. From sandy deserts to icy plains and choppy sea landings, there was a vehicle for every kind of terrain.

Daimler Scout Car "Dingo"

Produced in: UK

Speed: up to 95kph (59mph)

Weapons: 1 machine gun

Small, fast, protected by an inch-thick steel body and equipped with a powerful, long-range radio set, the Dingo could carry two soldiers on stealthy reconnaissance missions across dangerous territory.

BSA M20

Produced in: UK

Speed: 90kph (56mph)

Weapons: a rifle could be strapped on

The BSA (Birmingham Small Arms Company) M20 bike was slow and heavy, but could support a sidecar and tackle the roughest roads. Designed for delivering messages and escorting convoys, it was used in battle zones everywhere.

DUKW

Produced in: USA

Speed: 80kph (50mph) on road, 10kph (6mph) on water

Weapons: 1 machine gun on some

DUKWs, also known as "ducks," had waterproof bodies, propellers and six wheels. They could ferry heavy loads across water, roads and open country. Over 20,000 were built.

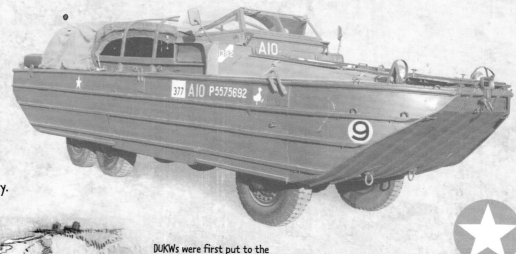

DUKWs were first put to the test when the Allies invaded Sicily in July 1943. They were so successful that they played a key part in Allied invasions from then on.

Dodge WC54 Ambulance

Produced in: USA

Speed: 80kph (50mph)

The Dodge WC54 used four-wheel drive power from its engine to reach wounded soldiers, no matter how wild the battlefield terrain. It carried a driver, doctor and bunk beds for up to four patients. The ambulance was daubed in Red Cross symbols to show it was being used to help the wounded.

"Jeep"

Produced in: USA

Speed: 70kph (44mph)

Weapons: fixings for machine gun

Off-road vehicles designed for scouting missions, jeeps were a tremendous success, with over half a million produced. They could be used anywhere – to cross shallow rivers, bounce over hills and ruts or carry a stretcher – and they were light enough to be loaded onto gliders and planes.

Kubelwagen

Produced in: Germany

Speed: 80kph (50mph)

Ugly, flimsy-looking and limited to two-wheel drive, the Kubelwagen was still an impressive transport vehicle – the German equivalent of the Allies' jeeps. Designed by Ferdinand Porsche, it was fast enough to keep up with tracked machines such as tanks.

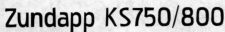

The Kubelwagen had a smooth underside so that it could slide across deep mud, snow or sand.

Zundapp KS750/800

Produced in: Germany

Speed: 95kph (59mph)

Weapons: sidecar mount for machine gun

The Zundapp's engine powered the outer wheel of its sidecar, making it a formidable cross-country vehicle for up to three soldiers. It was also strong enough to pull a small trailer loaded with weapons.

11

Warships

The ships used in Second World War navies were floating fortresses with thick metal hulls and massive guns. But they faced extinction during the War, because of attacks by submarines and bomber aircraft.

Admiral Graf Spee

Crew: 1,100
Launched: 1934
Length: 186m (610ft)
Firepower: 6 x 280mm (11") diameter guns, 8 x 150mm (5.9") guns
Speed: 28 knots (52kph / 32mph)

This German "pocket" battleship sank British merchant ships but was badly damaged in December 1939 in a fight with three British cruisers. The captain gave orders to scuttle (sink) his own ship.

HMS Belfast

Crew: 950
Launched: 1938
Length: 187m (614ft)
Firepower: 12 x 150mm (5.9") guns, 8 x 100mm (3.9") guns
Speed: 32 knots (59kph / 37mph)

The *Belfast* was a medium-sized British cruiser that protected convoys heading to the Soviet Union, and later supported the D-Day landings in Normandy.
Today, it's a museum ship moored on the River Thames in London.

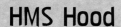

British navy flag

HMS Hood

Crew: 1,418
Launched: 1918
Length: 260m (853ft)
Firepower: 8 x 380mm (15") guns, 14 x 100mm (3.9") guns
Speed: 28 knots (52kph / 32mph)

The "mighty *Hood*" was the pride of the British Royal Navy, but the battlecruiser was old and poorly protected. During a fight with the Germans' best warship – *Bismarck* – in May 1941, the *Hood* exploded, broke in two and sank within seconds. Only three sailors survived.

Yamato

Crew: 2,300
Launched: 1940
Length: 260m (853ft)

Firepower: 9 x 450mm (17.7")
guns, 6 x 150mm (5.9") guns
Speed: 27 knots (50kph / 31mph)

Using two huge catapults, the *Yamato* could launch planes to seek out enemy ships nearby.

The Japanese *Yamato* was the biggest, most heavily-armed ship ever built. But, by the Second World War, even giant ships were at threat from bombers launched by enemy carriers. The *Yamato* was sunk in 1945 by US planes, and almost all its crew died.

USS Missouri

US navy flag

Crew: up to 3,000
Launched: 1944
Length: 270m (886ft)
Firepower: 9 x 410mm (16.1")
guns and 20 x 120mm (4.7") guns
Speed: 33 knots (61kph / 38mph)

The *Missouri* fought in the Pacific Ocean against the Japanese fleet. The Second World War officially ended on its decks, when Japanese officials signed a document of surrender in September 1945.

HMS Ark Royal

Crew: up to 1,600
Launched: 1937
Length: 240m (787ft)

Firepower: up to 60 planes, 16 x 140mm
(5.5") guns, dozens of anti-aircraft guns
Speed: 31 knots (57kph / 36mph)

Fast enough to outpace most enemy ships, the British aircraft carrier *Ark Royal* held up to 60 planes below its decks. It demonstrated the importance of air power in the war at sea, but was sunk in late 1941 by a German submarine.

Fairey Swordfish torpedo planes from the *Ark Royal* helped to locate and sink the *Bismarck*.

Bismarck

Crew: 2,000
Launched: 1939
Length: 250m (820ft)

Firepower: 8 x 380mm (15")
guns, 12 x 150mm (5.9") guns
Speed: 30 knots (56kph / 35mph)

Bismarck was a huge German warship. It was such a threat that the British Prime Minister, Winston Churchill, ordered the Royal Navy to destroy it at any cost. It sank in 1941, after being bombarded by ships and planes launched from the *Ark Royal*.

Submarines

During the Second World War, submarines prowled the world's oceans, hidden beneath the waves. They blasted ships with explosive torpedoes, laid mines and ferried elite troops around on secret missions.

Submarine captains used periscopes, poking up above the waves, to spot enemy ships.

SM Surcouf

Nationality: French
Crew: 118
Launched: 1929

Length: 110m (361ft)
Speed: 18.5 knots (34kph / 21mph) on the surface / 10 knots (19kph / 12mph) when submerged

When it was built, the *Surcouf* was the biggest submarine ever constructed. Unlike most other subs in the Second World War, it sometimes carried prisoners captured from enemy ships. It sank with its entire crew after a collision with an American merchant ship in 1942.

The *Surcouf* had two gigantic guns, like the ones which were fitted onto heavy warships.

Type VII

Nationality: German

Crew: 52

Launched: 1941

Length: 67m (220ft)

Speed: 17.6 knots (33kph / 20mph) / 7.7 knots (14kph / 9mph)

Each Type VII submarine had a small deck gun in front of its turret, to use above water.

German submarines were known as U-boats (short for *Unterseeboote*). They hunted in groups, intercepting convoys of Allied ships in the Atlantic Ocean and attacking at night on the surface. These "wolf packs," as they became known, sank almost 3,000 British merchant ships. Over 700 Type VII U-boats fought in the War – more than any other type of submarine.

Submarines sank merchant ships using underwater missiles called torpedoes.

Gato Class

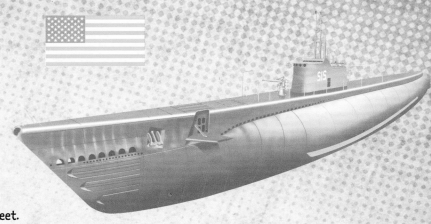

Nationality: American

Crew: 60

Launched: 1943

Length: up to 95m (311ft)

Speed: 21 knots (39kph / 24mph) / 9 knots (17kph / 10mph)

The United States sent fewer than 260 submarines to patrol the Pacific Ocean, but they destroyed over half of Japan's merchant fleet and sank many large warships. Gato Class ships, named after a small type of shark, made up the backbone of the US submarine fleet.

Maiale

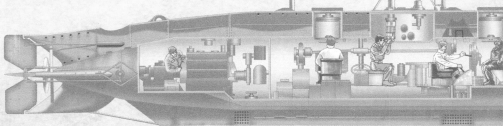

Nationality: Italian

Crew: 2

Launched: 1940

Length: 7.3m (24ft)

Speed: 4.5 knots (8kph / 5mph)

These "human torpedoes" were launched from bigger submarines. The riders steered towards enemy ships, cutting through protective netting if necessary. Then, they attached explosives to the hull, before escaping back to their submarine.

X-Craft

Nationality: British

Crew: 4

Launched: 1942

Length: 15m

Speed: 6 knots (11kph / 7mph) / 5 knots (9kph / 6mph)

These "midget" subs were small enough to sneak through narrow waterways, cut through torpedo nets and attack enemy warships at anchor. X-Craft also helped to investigate German defenses near the Normandy beaches before the D-Day landings.

X-Craft carried divers to perform underwater missions. One was James Joseph Magennis, who won the Victoria Cross for successfully attaching mines to a Japanese ship in July 1945. First though, he had to scrape seaweed and barnacles off the ship's hull.

War posters

Very few families owned a television set during the War, so most governments relied on radio broadcasting and posters, with striking images and snappy messages, to remind everyone that they were fighting for their lives and their nation's future.

Winston Churchill, the British Prime Minster, was a bold, popular wartime leader. He urged the British people to fight to the death against invasion.

A picture of British Commonwealth soldiers reminded people in Britain that their troops were not fighting alone.

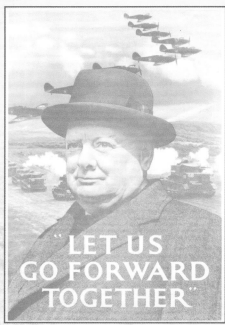

"LET US GO FORWARD TOGETHER"

TOGETHER

Women were encouraged to work in factories, producing weapons and ammunition for the men fighting overseas.

Even the King of England's daughter, the future Elizabeth II, trained as a mechanic, working on army vehicles.

WOMEN OF BRITAIN
COME INTO THE FACTORIES
ASK AT ANY EMPLOYMENT EXCHANGE FOR ADVICE AND FULL DETAILS

Some posters warned civilians to be on their guard for spies and saboteurs. More than a dozen enemy agents were caught trying to enter Britain.

You never know who's listening!

CARELESS TALK COSTS LIVES

Some nations used shocking images to portray enemy soldiers as savage beasts. This Russian poster makes a single, chilling demand – *Take Revenge*.

Governments wanted to persuade every civilian that they had a vital part to play in the struggle for victory.

EVERY CANADIAN MUST FIGHT

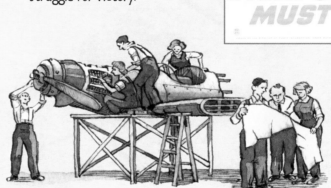

Civilians who had never worked in factories before were trained to put together complicated equipment, such as planes.

War is expensive. The US Government raised cash by selling war bonds – savings stamps – to the public. Movie stars and medal-winning soldiers held rallies to encourage people to buy. Among them were soldiers from this poster. The image is based on a famous photograph of the men raising the US flag on the Japanese island of Iwo Jima.

This is the cover of sheet music for a famous Second World War song, "We'll meet again." It shows a soldier waving goodbye to his sweetheart – a poignant image at a time when many soldiers never came home again.

WE'LL MEET AGAIN

Words & Music by
ROSS PARKER and
HUGHIE CHARLES

JOE LOSS
AND HIS BAND

6ᴰ

7th
WAR LOAN
NOW··ALL TOGETHER

"We'll meet again" was one of the most popular songs sung by Vera Lynn, a singer who often went abroad to give performances for British troops.

D-Day

On June 6, 1944 the largest invasion force ever assembled stormed into
Norman... ...nce. Codenamed "D-Day," it was a huge gamble
for the ... ...t failed, tens of thousands of troops might have died
and the ...lied war effort ... ...ve been derailed for years.

CHERBOURG

"UTAH" BEACH
(U...

"OMAHA" BEACH
(...US)

...OINTE
DU HOC

⑤

MAP GUIDE

	land won on D-Day
	main town
	pillbox (guard post)
	beach obstacles
	coastal guns
	German tanks

The Allies marked their planes
with black and white stripes
so Allied troops on the
ground would recognize them.
Watch out for these stripes
on the stickers!

ST-LÔ

NORMANDY

But months of planning, along with the bravery of individual soldiers, helped the Allies fight their way off the beaches and into Europe. After the success of D-Day, many German generals gave up hope of winning the war.

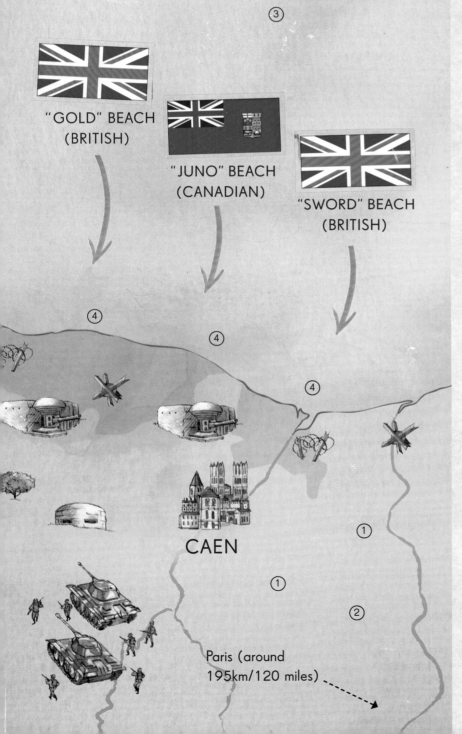

Match the stickers to these numbers on the map.
③

③

"GOLD" BEACH
(BRITISH)

"JUNO" BEACH
(CANADIAN)

"SWORD" BEACH
(BRITISH)

④

④

④

①

CAEN

①

②

Paris (around
195km/120 miles)

D-DAY TIMELINE

From **00:00** British and Canadian paratroopers land to the east of the beach codenamed *Sword*, while US paratroopers land to the west of *Utah* beach. They seize bridges, exits and strongholds. Then, weapons and vehicles are carried over in gliders.

Paratroopers ①   Gliders ②

05:00 The Germans open fire on approaching Allied ships. Allied ships bombard the defending Germans.

Battleships ③

06:30 A small US unit scales a cliff to capture German coastal guns at Pointe du Hoc. Larger US forces land on *Utah* and *Omaha* beaches. *Utah* Beach is secured within 3 hours, but by the end of a day of fighting and bloodshed, the Allies have no more than a few footholds on *Omaha* beach.

07:30 British troops land on *Gold* and *Sword* beaches. *Gold* Beach is secured within hours. By midday the troops have begun marching inland.

07:45 Canadian troops land on *Juno* beach. It's well-defended, but by the afternoon they've fought their way inland.

Landing crafts ④

Throughout the day, bombers fly in over the rest of Normandy, hitting important targets such as railways.

Allied bombers ⑤

By nightfall, over 150,000 Allied troops have landed, with a loss of around 12,000 men.
In less than a year, Hitler will be defeated.

War stories

The Second World War inspired many acts of courage and determination from soldiers and civilians on both sides. Here are the stories of a few of these extraordinary men and women.

Douglas Bader

Douglas Bader lost both legs in an accident in the 1930s, but he soon proved that, even with prosthetic legs, he was still a gifted pilot. He was taken on by the RAF and shot down more than 20 German fighters, until he was shot down himself in 1941 and spent more than three years as a prisoner of war (POW). When the War ended, he led around 300 RAF planes in a victory flight over London.

Pavlichenko was awarded the "Gold Star of the Hero of the Soviet Union" medal – the highest award in the Red Army.

Lyudmila Pavlichenko

The Soviet Union was the only nation in the War to encourage women to fight on the front line. Major Lyudmila Pavlichenko was a sniper in the "Red Army" – the Soviet land force. She was an expert shot who stalked war-torn cities with a rifle, picking off enemy soldiers.

Erwin Rommel

A brilliant commander, Erwin Rommel led the German forces in North Africa to several stunning victories. He was a fierce soldier, but treated prisoners and civilians well. Late in the War, he decided Hitler was leading Germany to ruin, and plotted to overthrow him.

Bernard Montgomery

Bernard Montgomery was the British general who finally defeated Rommel's forces in Africa. A strong-willed man, known for his trademark black beret, "Monty" later helped lead the Allies to victory in western Europe, as commander of ground forces during D-Day (see pages 18-19).

Charles Upham

Britain's top military medal, the Victoria Cross, was awarded to fewer than 200 soldiers in the War. But one New Zealander – Charles Upham – received it twice: for his actions in Crete in 1941, and in Egypt in 1942. On both occasions, he showed incredible bravery, even after being wounded.

The Victoria Cross

Murphy plays a cowboy in a Western film.

Audie Murphy

Baby-faced, short and slim, the teenage Audie Murphy didn't look like much of a soldier when he arrived at army training camp. But he won more medals than any other US serviceman in the War, including the Medal of Honor, America's top military award. Murphy's good looks helped him to become a movie star in the 1950s.

Claus von Stauffenberg

In 1944, a group of German officers, including von Stauffenberg and Rommel, tried to overthrow Hitler and end the War. Von Stauffenberg planted a bomb at a meeting Hitler was attending, but though the explosion killed several people, Hitler escaped almost unharmed. Von Stauffenberg and many of his supporters were executed.

Von Stauffenberg had been badly injured in Africa in 1943, losing an eye and a hand.

Anne Frank kept a diary while in hiding. Published after the War, it's now one of the most widely-read books in the world.

Anne Frank

In the 1930s, Hitler began persecuting Jews and other minority groups. Later, the Germans built concentration camps across Europe, where they murdered millions of people. But some Jewish families managed to hide. Anne Frank was 13 years old when her family moved into secret rooms in Amsterdam. For two years, she lived in fear – until they were discovered. She died in a camp, months before the War ended.

A history of the War

As dawn broke on September 1, 1939, German forces thundered into Poland. So began the Second World War, the deadliest conflict in history. The fighting spread across the globe, as powerful nations formed two opposing alliances – the Axis and the Allies.

The outbreak of war is announced in London.

Europe at war

From 1938, Adolf Hitler, the ambitious dictator of Germany, began to expand his country's territory. But when the German army invaded Poland in 1939, the British and French governments decided that Hitler had gone too far. They declared war on Germany.

Blitzkrieg!

The following year, Hitler launched a series of rapid strikes on western Europe, known as *Blitzkrieg*. By the end of June 1940, his troops had occupied Denmark, Norway, Holland, Belgium and France. By summer 1941, most of Europe was under German control. Meanwhile, Italy and Japan joined Germany to form the Axis Powers.

German troops march through Paris to celebrate their victory in France.

The London skyline, clogged with smoke from German bombs

Battle for Britain

After defeating the French, Hitler sent his air force, the *Luftwaffe*, to destroy Britain's RAF (Royal Air Force). This would clear the way for his army to invade.

But his plan failed, thanks to the fierce resistance of the RAF. Hitler gave up on his invasion plans, and the *Luftwaffe* turned to bombing British towns and cities instead.

German soldiers in snow camouflage in the Soviet Union

Into Russia

Hitler had made a peace treaty with Josef Stalin, ruler of the Soviet Union (formerly the Russian empire). But, in 1941, Hitler sent his army to invade. At first the Germans were successful, but over the next three years the Soviets fought back, forcing the invaders to retreat.

Pearl Harbor

Meanwhile, the Japanese were aggressively expanding their empire across the Pacific Ocean. On December 7, 1941, they bombed a US naval base at Pearl Harbor in Hawaii.

Enraged, the Americans joined Britain and the Soviet Union to form the Allied Powers. But the Japanese empire kept expanding through southeast Asia, almost as far as Australia.

Japanese bombs fall on Pearl Harbor in Hawaii.

Desert duel

Armies clashed in the deserts of North Africa, too, where the British and Italians had colonies. British Commonwealth forces won some early victories, until Hitler sent German forces to help. But, by 1942, the Axis forces were running low on equipment and fuel, and the Allies gained the upper hand.

D-Day

By 1944, the Germans had been beaten in North Africa, their invasion of the Soviet Union had failed, and Italy had surrendered.

On June 6, the Allies launched a huge invasion of France, known as "D-Day." A massive army of Allied troops landed on the beaches of Normandy. They defeated the Germans there and began to push inland into Europe. Meanwhile, the Soviet army advanced on Germany from the east.

Allied troops disembark from landing vessels to storm beaches in Normandy.

The end of the War

In April 1945, Soviet forces attacked Berlin. Hitler committed suicide, and on May 7, Germany surrendered. People celebrated throughout Europe. Meanwhile, US, British and Commonwealth troops were still battling against Japan. In August, after months of fighting over islands in the Pacific, the US dropped two deadly atomic bombs on Japan. They killed tens of thousands, forcing the Japanese government to surrender. Finally, the Second World War was over.

You can find out more about the Second World War by going to the Usborne Quicklinks Website
at www.usborne-quicklinks.com and typing in the keywords "second world war sticker book".

Acknowledgements

Cover: t © Antony Nettle / Alamy, mr IWM E18980, b IWM IWM-SITE-LAM-000472; p2: t IWM TR139, m IWM COL186, b IWM 2010.200.1; p3: t © Trustees of the RAF Museum / Iain Duncan, m © Parallax Photography / CORBIS, b © Museum of Flight / CORBIS; p4: t © Trustees of the RAF Museum / Iain Duncan, b © Trustees of the RAF Museum / Iain Duncan; p5: t IWM AIR.095.003.2, tm IWM 2010.20.3.1, bm © Trustees of the RAF Museum / Iain Duncan, b IWM DUX_T_96_79_56; p6: t IWM 4000.50.2, b IWM 4800.60.2.1; p7: t IWM DUX-T-88-37-16, tm © The Tank Museum, Bovington, bm IWM 4100.95.1, b © The Tank Museum, Bovington; p8-9: all pictures, © The Tank Museum, Bovington; p10: t © The Tank Museum, Bovington, m IWM 4110.30.1, b © The Tank Museum, Bovington; p11: t IWM 4008.28.1, tm IWM 4007.50.2, bm © idp show collection / Alamy, b © Bernie Epstein / Alamy; p12: t © Photos 12 / Alamy, m IWM IWM-SITE-BELF-000346, b IWM Q83329; p13: t © Koichi Kamoshida / Getty Images Entertainment / Getty Images, tm © CORBIS, bm © National Museum of the Royal Navy, b © akg-images / ullstein bild; p16: tl IWM PST14971, bl IWM PST3645, tr IWM PST3158, br IWM PST0142; p17: tl IWM PST0782, bl © Swim Ink 2, LLC / CORBIS, tr IWM PST8242, br © Mary Evans Picture Library / Alamy; p20: t IWM CH1406, ml © RIA Novosti / Topfoto, mr © RIA Novosti / Alamy, bl IWM HU5625, br IWM E18980; p21: tl IWM E6066, tr IWM OMD5379, tm © Bettmann/CORBIS, bm © CORBIS, b © Pictorial Press Ltd / Alamy; p22: t IWM NYP22535, b © CORBIS; p23: t IWM OEM6631, b IWM B5103

IWM = Courtesy of the Trustees of the Imperial War Museum

For more information about the Imperial War Museum, go to www.iwm.org.uk

With thanks to Ruth King and Sam Noonan

Additional illustration by Giovanni Paulli
Digital manipulation by John Russell

First published in 2011 by Usborne Publishing Ltd.

Original edition published in association with the Imperial War Museum

ISBN 978-0-545-43366-2

12 11 10 9 8 7 6 5 4 3 2 1   12 13 14 15 16 17/0

Printed in Malaysia   106

This edition first printing, January 2012